Cursed Grounds

by Steven L. Stern

Consultant: Paul F. Johnston
Washington, D.C.

BEARPORT PUBLISHING

New York, New York

Credits

Cover and Title Page, © Alexey Rodkin/Shutterstock, © Dennis Donohue/Shutterstock, and Florian ISPAS/Shutterstock; 6L, © Speaking Picture/India Picture/Photolibrary; 6R, © Shahnawaz Sid; 7, © Frédéric Soltan/Corbis; 8, © Paul Dymond/Alamy; 9L, © Newspix/News Ltd/Anna Rogers; 9R, © Paul Dymond/Lonely Planet/Newscom; 10, © Shropshire Star; 11T, © kostakirov/Shutterstock; 11C, © simpleman/Shutterstock; 11B, © Igor Kovalchuk/Shutterstock; 12, © Vienna Report Agency/Sygma/Corbis; 13TL, © AP Images/Winfried Rothermel; 13TR, © AP Images/Petr David Josek; 13B, © South Tyrol Museum of Archaeology, Bolzano, Italy/Wolfgang Neeb/The Bridgeman Art Library International; 14L, © Fotosearch/SuperStock; 14R, © Nora Bibel/laif/Redux; 15, © James Cheadle/Alamy; 16, © Tui De Roy/Minden Pictures/NGS Images; 17, © Hannamariah/Shutterstock; 18, © Jeff Belanger/Ghostvillage.com; 20, © Hal Sherman; 21T, © Bettmann/Corbis; 21B, © Scott Beveridge; 22, © John N. Weiss; 23L, © David B. King; 23R, © Jeff Greenberg/Alamy; 24, © Yamhill County Historical Society; 25T, © moritorus/Shutterstock; 25B, © Randy Kashka; 26, © Thomas Barrat/Shutterstock; 27, From Chicago Tribune, © June 25, 1960 All rights reserved. Used by permission and protected by the Copyright Laws of the United States; 31, © bumihills/Shutterstock.

Publisher: Kenn Goin
Editorial Director: Adam Siegel
Creative Director: Spencer Brinker
Design: Dawn Beard Creative
Cover: Kim Jones
Photo Researcher: Omni-Photo Communications, Inc.

Library of Congress Cataloging-in-Publication Data

Stern, Steven L.
  Cursed grounds / by Steven L. Stern.
     p. cm. — (Scary places)
  Includes bibliographical references and index.
  ISBN-13: 978-1-61772-147-2 (library binding)
  ISBN-10: 1-61772-147-6 (library binding)
  1. Haunted places—Juvenile literature. I. Title.
  BF1461.S48 2011
  133.1'2—dc22
                              2010041162

For more information, write to Bearport Publishing Company, Inc., 101 Fifth Avenue, Suite 6R, New York, New York 10003. Printed in the United States of America in North Mankato, Minnesota.

122010
10810CGF

10 9 8 7 6 5 4 3 2 1

Contents

Cursed Grounds

There are parts of the world that seem to be under a dark **spell**. According to some, these **cursed** places have the power to cause injury, disaster, and even death. How did these places become doomed? Some have been cursed by spoken words. Others seem by their very nature to be places of great misfortune.

Among the 11 cursed places in this book, you'll discover a ruined city that people are afraid to enter, a rocky creek where a dead woman's **spirit** is said to draw swimmers to their deaths, and the frozen grave of a man who lived more than 5,000 years ago. Are all of these places truly cursed? Read on and decide for yourself.

The Wizard's Curse

Bhangarh, India

Built in the late 1500s, the beautiful city of Bhangarh (BAHN-gar) once bustled with more than 10,000 people. Today its **ruins** are all that remain—except for the ghosts. No one dares to enter the city after dark. In fact, the government itself has posted a sign warning people to keep out.

A temple in Bhangarh

भारत सरकार
भारतीय पुरातत्व सर्वेक्षण, भानगढ़
आवश्यक सूचना—(1) भानगढ़ की सीमा में सूर्योदय से पहले एवं सूर्यास्त के पश्चात प्रवेश वर्जित है ।
(2) भानगढ़ की सीमा में किसी भी प्रकार के मवेशियों का प्रवेश कराना कानूनन अपराध है, आज्ञा का उल्लंघन करने पर कानूनी कार्यवाही की जावेगी ।
(3) भानगढ़ की सीमा में केवड़े के वृक्ष भारतीय पुरातत्व सर्वेक्षण विभाग (भारत सरकार की सम्पत्ती है । केवड़े के वृक्षों को किसी भी प्रकार की क्षति पहुँचाना मना है ।
नोट:- उपरोक्त आदेशों का उल्लंघन करने पर कानूनी कार्यवाही की जावेगी ।
आज्ञा से
"अधीक्षक पुरातत्व विद्"

This sign warns people to keep out of Bhangarh before sunrise and after sunset.

According to **legend**, Bhangarh's troubles began hundreds of years ago when an evil wizard spied a beautiful princess. To make her fall in love with him, the wizard created a magic love **potion**. However, before he could use the potion, the princess learned what the wizard had done. She grabbed the bowl that held the potion and smashed it against a boulder, causing the huge rock to roll over the wizard and crush him to death.

As the wizard lay dying, he cursed Bhangarh. He said that the city would be destroyed and no one would live there again. The wizard's **curse** soon came to pass. Bhangarh and its people were wiped out in a war with neighboring Ajabgarh (AH-jab-gar).

By 1783, the beautiful city was completely abandoned. To this day, no one has come to live in the crumbling buildings left behind. Perhaps that is because, as some visitors claim, the ghosts of those who died in Bhangarh remain there today.

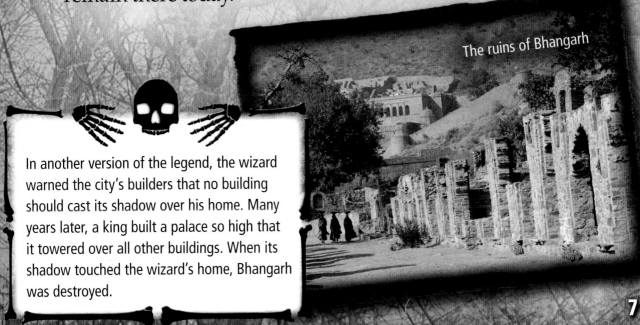

The ruins of Bhangarh

In another version of the legend, the wizard warned the city's builders that no building should cast its shadow over his home. Many years later, a king built a palace so high that it towered over all other buildings. When its shadow touched the wizard's home, Bhangarh was destroyed.

The Devil's Pool

Babinda Creek, Queensland, Australia

What is legend? What is fact? Is a rocky creek in northeastern Australia just a dangerous place to swim, or is it a cursed place that claims the lives of those who dare to intrude?

Deep in an Australian **rain forest** flow the cool, clear waters of Babinda Creek. It is a beautiful setting, yet one that is filled with danger.

Babinda Creek

According to legend, many years ago a young **Aborigine** woman named Oolana married Waroonoo, an older man from her tribe. Not long after they married, Oolana met a young man named Dyga from another tribe. The two fell instantly in love and ran away together.

People from both tribes chased after the young couple. They captured them near Babinda Creek. To escape, Oolana threw herself into the fast-moving waters, where she drowned. Many say her spirit remains in the creek's swirling depths.

Since 1959, at least 17 people have drowned in what is now called the Devil's Pool. All but one of the **victims** were male. Those who have survived the chilling waters talk of a force pulling them under. Could it be Oolana's ghost, dragging young men down in the hopes that one might be her true love Dyga?

A warning sign for swimmers at Babinda Creek

Strange photos have been taken at the Devil's Pool. For example, the father of a drowned man photographed the place where his son had fallen into the water. When the picture was developed, the young man's face appeared on the rocks.

The deep waters of Babinda Creek are surprisingly cold.

Last Words of an Innocent Man

Condover Hall, Shropshire, England

Today, Condover Hall is a beautiful **mansion** in the English countryside. About 500 years ago, however, it was the scene of murder, lies, and a dead man's curse.

Condover Hall

In the 1500s, Lord Knyvett (NYE-vet) owned the grand Condover Hall and the surrounding land. One dark night, Lord Knyvett's son crept up to his father as he slept, and stabbed him. Knyvett stumbled out of the room, crying for help. His wound was too deep for him to live, though. Knyvett fell to the ground, dead.

The evil son blamed a servant named John Viam for his father's murder. Viam insisted he was innocent, but no one believed him and he was hanged. Before he was killed, however, Viam spoke these words: "I am innocent, though my master's son swears me **guilty**. And as I **perish** an innocent man, may those who follow my murdered lord be cursed."

Viam's wish came true. Neither Knyvett's son nor anyone related to him ever had good fortune in Condover Hall. In fact, after Viam's death, Knyvett's son was eventually found guilty of his father's murder—and hanged.

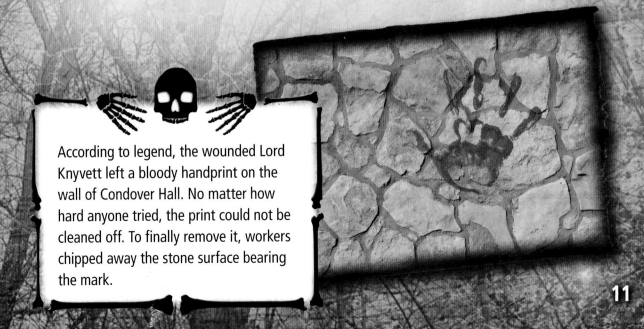

According to legend, the wounded Lord Knyvett left a bloody handprint on the wall of Condover Hall. No matter how hard anyone tried, the print could not be cleaned off. To finally remove it, workers chipped away the stone surface bearing the mark.

Curse of the Iceman

Ötztal Alps, between Italy and Austria

Some places are best left undisturbed. Perhaps one of these is the icy grave of a hunter who bled to death from an arrow wound more than 5,000 years ago. Did removing the hunter's frozen body from his resting place high in the Alps set a curse in motion? The deaths of seven people seem to suggest so.

In 1991, Helmut Simon and his wife stumbled onto a frozen body while hiking in the Ötztal (UHRTS-tol) Alps. Many thought it was the **remains** of an unlucky mountain climber. However, when scientists studied the body, they discovered the shocking truth. It was the **mummy** of a man who had lived around 3300 B.C.

The frozen body found by Helmut Simon and his wife

Scientists learned all sorts of things about **prehistoric** life by studying the mummy, whom people named "Ötzi (UHRT-see) the Iceman." For example, Ötzi had worn shoes made from the skins of deer and bears. He had stuffed them with grass to keep his feet warm.

As time passed, whispers about a curse connected to Ötzi began. First a leading scientist who had examined the Iceman died in a car crash. Then a mountain guide who had taken people to the site of the Iceman's remains was killed in an **avalanche**. Helmut Simon, the hiker who had found the body, fell 300 feet (91 m) to his death during a blizzard. Before long, a total of seven people who'd had close contact with Ötzi were dead. Could a curse from the Iceman have killed them?

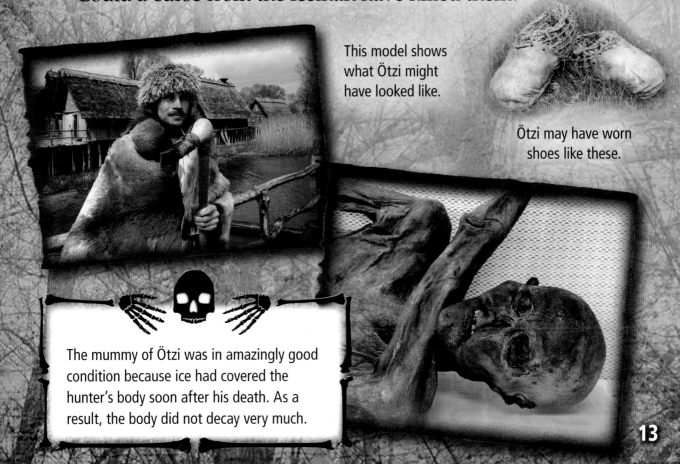

This model shows what Ötzi might have looked like.

Ötzi may have worn shoes like these.

The mummy of Ötzi was in amazingly good condition because ice had covered the hunter's body soon after his death. As a result, the body did not decay very much.

A Haunted Highway

Highway 191, Utah

Highway 191 was once part of Route 666—a well-traveled highway that ran through parts of Arizona, Utah, New Mexico, and Colorado. Today, however, one lonely stretch of this road is more well known for frightening drivers.

Highway 191

Late one night, a man was driving on Highway 191. There wasn't another car to be seen for miles. Then suddenly, from out of nowhere, he saw a truck barreling down the middle of the road toward him. Sparks flew from the wheels and flames poured from the smokestack. The man had to pull over so he wouldn't get run off the road.

The terrifying trucker isn't the only deadly force on this highway. Native Americans claim that **medicine men** may appear there as well. Using their magical powers, they can change into animals, such as crows, coyotes, or wolves. Sometimes they cause cars to crash by suddenly appearing in the middle of the road.

According to some, other mysterious creatures have also been spotted on the highway. Packs of evil ghost dogs are said to have attacked cars that stopped on the road. They shred the cars' tires with their sharp teeth. So if someday you are on Highway 191 at night, don't stop, and watch out for strange vehicles on this cursed road!

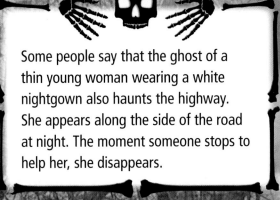

Some people say that the ghost of a thin young woman wearing a white nightgown also haunts the highway. She appears along the side of the road at night. The moment someone stops to help her, she disappears.

Cursed in the Middle of the Sea

Palmyra Atoll, Pacific Ocean

Something evil **lurks** around Palmyra (pal-MYE-ruh) **Atoll**—and it's not the vicious sharks that are known to attack people who swim in the shallow waters near shore. The sharks' sharp teeth are frightening—but not nearly as scary as Palmyra itself.

Palmyra Atoll

Palmyra Atoll sits about 1,000 miles (1,609 km) south of Hawaii. The cursed atoll was first discovered in 1798 when an American sailor nearly crashed his ship into Palmyra's sharp **reefs**. In the years that followed, other sailors were not so lucky. Several ships were wrecked in the atoll's deadly reefs. No one on board survived the sea and the sharks.

During World War II (1939–1945), the United States used Palmyra as a landing strip for airplanes. However, some planes crashed or mysteriously vanished near the atoll without a trace. When asked about one of these lost planes, a navy officer said that it seemed like it had "dropped off the edge of the earth."

Years later, in 1974, a couple from California sailed to Palmyra, hoping to have a pleasant time there. Unfortunately, a man who wanted their boat and food was living on the atoll—and he killed them. The couple became two more victims of the Palmyra curse.

Six years after the murder, the skull and bones of one of the murder victims washed up onshore. No remains of the other victim have ever been found.

The Dudleytown Curse

Dudleytown, Connecticut

In northwestern Connecticut lies the village of Dudleytown. For hundreds of years, a few families tried to make a living by farming the rocky soil there, yet fires, deaths, disappearances, and **insanity** have led many to think the village is cursed.

The woods of Dudleytown

In 1510, Edmund Dudley was **beheaded** in England for plotting against the king. That was when a curse was said to have been put on the Dudley family. This curse supposedly followed the family to Connecticut, where some of its members settled in the 1700s.

Some people don't believe the curse exists. Yet bad luck and strange events have surrounded Dudleytown. Perhaps the first victim was Abiel Dudley, who went insane before he died in 1799. Other strange and violent deaths in the village followed, including one in which a woman was hit by lightning while standing on her front porch.

By the late 1800s, nearly everyone had fled Dudleytown. One man who remained was John Brophy, who soon felt the curse as well. First his wife died. Shortly after the **funeral**, his two children disappeared in the forest. Then his house burned down. Brophy himself later vanished without a trace.

Before long, Dudleytown became a ghost town. Today, curious visitors are drawn there by reports of restless spirits and other strange sights and sounds. Some have even claimed that invisible hands touched them in Dudleytown's dark and silent woods.

In the 1920s, a doctor and his wife built a vacation home in the Dudleytown area. The doctor was called to New York for an emergency. When he returned the next day, his wife had gone mad. She **babbled** about strange creatures coming out of the woods.

Chief Cornstalk's Revenge

Point Pleasant, West Virginia

Chief Cornstalk was a great leader of the Shawnee Indians. A fierce warrior, he was respected by friends and feared by his enemies. Did the bloody murder of the chief and his son bring death and disaster to a town in West Virginia?

Chief Cornstalk

POINT PLEASANT

Fort Blair was built here in 1774 and later Fort Randolph, the center of Indian activities, 1777-1778. Here are graves of "Mad Anne" Bailey, border scout, and Cornstalk, Shawnee chief, held hostage and killed here in 1777.

In 1777, Chief Cornstalk went to a **fort** in what is now known as Point Pleasant, West Virginia. Cornstalk wanted to speak with the army captain to prevent fighting between **Native Americans** and **colonists**. However, while Cornstalk was at the fort, two soldiers were attacked in the woods.

Even though the attackers were not Shawnee, the other soldiers turned on Cornstalk. They murdered his son and shot Cornstalk eight times. With his dying breath, the chief cursed both the soldiers and the land.

Since then, the area around Point Pleasant has suffered fires, floods, and mysterious disasters. In 1907, more than 300 coal miners died in a mining tragedy. In 1967, the Silver Bridge suddenly collapsed into the Ohio River, killing 46 people. Soon after, there were two fatal plane crashes. Each new disaster seems to whisper a reminder of Chief Cornstalk's curse.

The collapse of Silver Bridge

Chief Cornstalk's curse has linked Point Pleasant to many strange legends and stories. Some say it is home to Mothman, a seven-foot-tall (2-m) creature with glowing red eyes and large wings. Some even blame Mothman for the Silver Bridge collapse.

This statue of Mothman stands in Point Pleasant, West Virginia.

Curse of the Three Sisters

Potomac River, Washington, D.C.

In the early 1600s, the Powhatan (pow-HAT-uhn) and Susquehannock (suhs-kwuh-HAN-uhk) Indians were deadly enemies. The Potomac (puh-TOH-muhk) River separated their lands. The killing of the Powhatan chief's three sons by the Susquehannocks led to a dark curse that still hangs over the river.

The Potomac River

Three Powhatan sisters were heartbroken when the men they had planned to marry were killed in battle against the Susquehannocks. They swore they would get **revenge** for these deaths. They set out across the Potomac River in a wooden raft. Unfortunately, the river's swift current and the blowing winds soon swept the sisters away.

Before they drowned, however, the women pronounced a curse. They said that if they could not cross the river at that place, no one ever would. According to legend, a terrible lightning storm then struck. By the time it was over, three small rocky islands had appeared in the river. These became known as the Three Sisters.

A statue of a Powhatan Indian

Since that time, many accidents and deaths have been blamed on the curse. Any effort to build a bridge in that place has failed. In 1972, the steel supports for a bridge were in place when a furious thunderstorm struck. When it ended, the steel skeleton had been destroyed. No one has dared try to build a bridge near the Three Sisters again.

The islands that became known as the Three Sisters

People have reported hearing moans and cries coming from the part of the river that is near the Three Sisters. It's said that the sounds may be a warning that the curse of the Three Sisters is about to claim another victim.

Fire, Fire, Fire

Lafayette, Oregon

Lafayette has had the rare misfortune of burning down not once but twice in its history. Why is the town so unlucky? Some say it is because of a bitter curse from a woman whose son was killed there.

Lafayette, Oregon

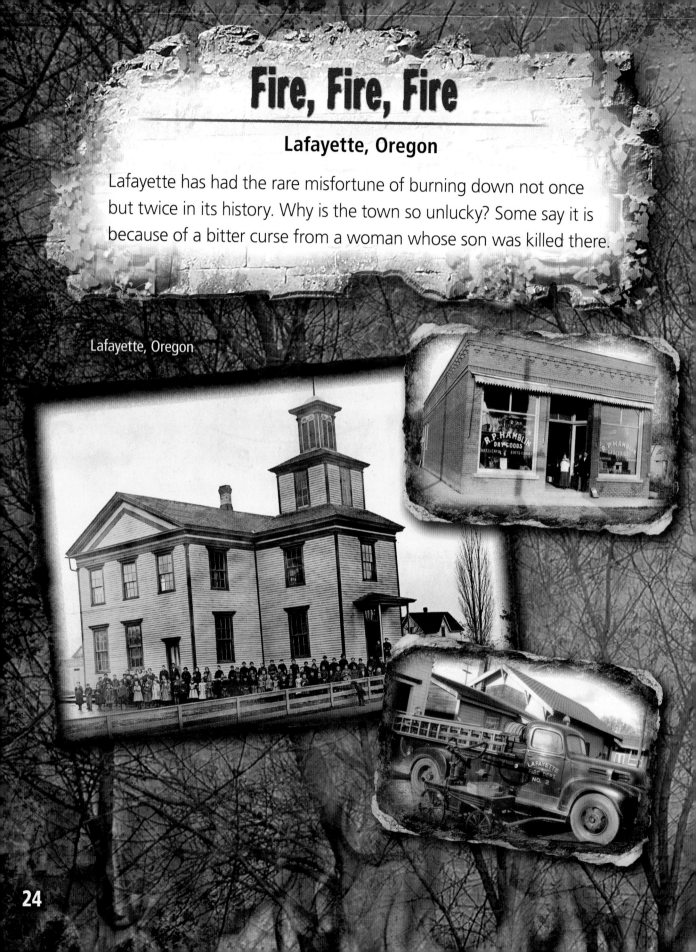

In 1886, Richard Marple was **accused** of brutally murdering a shopkeeper with an ax. Richard was tried, found guilty, and sentenced to death the following year. On the day of her son's hanging, the horribly upset and angry Anna Marple placed a curse on the town. She screamed that Lafayette would burn to the ground—not once, but three times.

In the years since then, two huge fires have indeed burned through the town. Will a third fire follow, as Anna Marple warned? Only time will tell.

Meanwhile, it's said that Anna's ghost haunts the Lafayette **cemetery** where her son is buried. People claim to have seen her walking there at night. Some have even said that they were chased by her ghost.

A cemetery in Lafayette, Oregon

Some people have reported discovering long scratch marks down their backs after visiting the cemetery. Are these marks left by thorny bushes—or are they scratches from an angry Anna Marple?

25

Curse of the Billy Goat

Wrigley Field, Chicago, Illinois

Not every curse leads to death and destruction. Fans of the Chicago Cubs baseball team know that some curses cause a different kind of pain. At first, people laughed at the so-called Billy Goat curse. As time passed, however, they could no longer deny its power.

Wrigley Field is the home stadium of the Chicago Cubs. This team was the first to win back-to-back World Series, in 1907 and 1908. Yet it has now been more than 100 years since the team has won a **title**.

Wrigley Field

How did the Cubs turn from a winning team into one doomed to lose? Their fate changed on October 6, 1945. The Cubs had already won two of the first three games of the World Series. William Sianis, owner of the Billy Goat Tavern, bought two tickets to the fourth game. Hoping to bring the Cubs luck, Sianis took Murphy, his pet goat, to Wrigley Field. However, he was told that animals were not allowed in the ballpark. Sianis pleaded with the Cubs' owner to let Murphy stay, but he refused. "The goat stinks!" the owner told him.

Sianis became so upset that he put a curse on the Cubs. He said, "The Cubs ain't gonna win no more. The Cubs will never win a World Series so long as the goat is not allowed in Wrigley Field." Since then, they never have.

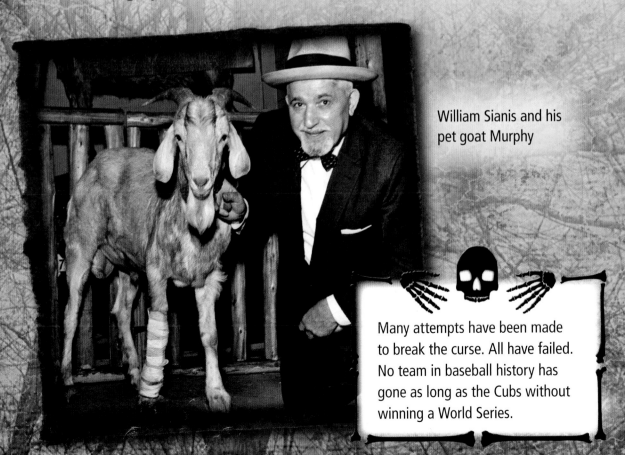

William Sianis and his pet goat Murphy

Many attempts have been made to break the curse. All have failed. No team in baseball history has gone as long as the Cubs without winning a World Series.

Cursed Grounds

Lafayette, Oregon

An angry mother promises destruction

Wrigley Field, Chicago, Illinois

A lingering curse still unbroken

Dudleytown, Connecticut

A village with a dark history

Potomac River, Washington, D.C.

A river cursed by three sisters

Point Pleasant, West Virginia

A bloody murder followed by a deadly curse

Highway 191, Utah

A lonely road with only ghosts for company

Palmyra Atoll, Pacific Ocean

An atoll of mystery and death

NORTH AMERICA

SOUTH AMERICA

Arctic Ocean

Pacific Ocean

Atlantic Ocean

Condover Hall, Shropshire, England

A beautiful mansion with a deadly past

ASIA

EUROPE

Ötztal Alps, between Italy and Austria

An ancient, icy grave

Pacific Ocean

AFRICA

Bhangarh, India

A haunted city of ruins

Indian Ocean

AUSTRALIA

Babinda Creek, Queensland, Australia

Chilling waters awaiting new victims

Southern Ocean

ANTARCTICA

Glossary

Aborigine (*ab*-uh-RIJ-uh-nee) a native person of Australia

accused (uh-KYOOZD) blamed for doing something wrong

atoll (AT-awl) a ring-shaped coral island that surrounds a lagoon

avalanche (AV-uh-lanch) a large amount of snow, ice, or rock that suddenly slides down a mountain

babbled (BAB-uhld) spoke excitedly and without making sense

beheaded (bih-HED-id) had one's head chopped off

cemetery (SEM-uh-ter-ee) an area of land where dead bodies are buried

colonists (KOL-uh-nists) people from another country who settle in an area and are ruled by the country from which they came

curse (KURSS) words spoken to cause evil or injury; a spell

cursed (KURST) under an evil spell and therefore likely to cause evil or injury

fort (FORT) a strong building from which people can defend an area

funeral (FYOO-nuh-ruhl) a ceremony that is held after a person dies

guilty (GIL-tee) having done something wrong or against the law

insanity (in-SAN-uh-tee) mental illness

legend (LEJ-uhnd) a story handed down from the past that may be based on fact but is not always completely true

lurks (LURKS) secretly hides or lies in wait

mansion (MAN-shuhn) a very large and grand house

medicine men (MED-uh-sin MEN) people thought to have magical powers to heal other people and control spirits

mummy (MUH-mee) the preserved body of a dead person or animal

Native Americans (NAY-tiv uh-MER-uh-kinz) the first people to live in America; they are sometimes called American Indians

perish (PAIR-ish) die

potion (POH-shuhn) a mixture of liquids

prehistoric (*pree*-hi-STOR-ik) before the time when people began to use writing to record history

rain forest (RAYN FOR-ist) a large, warm area of land covered with trees and plants, where lots of rain falls

reefs (REEFS) ridges of rocks, sand, or coral in the ocean near the water's surface

remains (ri-MAYNZ) all or part of a dead body

revenge (ri-VENJ) an act of getting even for something that has been unfairly done

ruins (ROO-inz) what is left of something that has decayed or been destroyed

spell (SPEL) spoken words that are supposed to have magical powers

spirit (SPIHR-it) a supernatural creature, such as a ghost

title (TYE-tuhl) the championship; in baseball a World Series win

victims (VIK-tuhmz) people who are hurt or killed by a person or an event

Bibliography

Cohen, Daniel. *Famous Curses.* New York: Dodd, Mead & Company (1979).

De Angelis, Gina. *It Happened in Washington, D.C.* Guilford, CT: The Globe Pequot Press (2004).

Hauck, Dennis William. *The International Directory of Haunted Places.* New York: Penguin Books (2000).

Read More

Banks, Cameron. *America's Most Haunted.* New York: Scholastic (2002).

Hamilton, John. *Haunted Places.* Edina, MN: ABDO Publishing Company (2007).

Holub, Joan. *The Haunted States of America.* New York: Aladdin (2001).

Learn More Online

To learn more about cursed places, visit
www.bearportpublishing.com/ScaryPlaces

Index

About the Author

Steven L. Stern has more than 30 years of experience as a writer and editor, developing textbooks, learning materials, and works of nonfiction and fiction for children and adults. He is the author of 23 books as well as numerous articles and short stories. He has also worked as a teacher, a lexicographer, and a writing consultant.